What IS a Map?

A map is a picture that shows where things are located or how they are related. It can show you where the houses are in your street, or where your country is in the world, or where the trees are in the park, or even where the stars are in the sky. Some are very simple, and some are very complicated indeed. Some people like to look at maps on rolls of paper, on their phones or computers, or in books—like this one!

For Lottie, Alice, Lana, and Emily Rose, with much love
xxx VF

To my mum
Y-LH

Text copyright © 2023 by Vivian French
Illustrations copyright © 2023 by Ya-Ling Huang

First edition 2023

Library of Congress Catalog Card Number 2022906996
ISBN 978-1-5362-2511-2

23 24 25 26 27 28 CCP 10 9 8 7 6 5 4 3 2

Printed in Shenzhen, Guangdong, China

This book was typeset in Anke Sans.
The illustrations were done in mixed media.

Candlewick Press
99 Dover Street
Somerville, Massachusetts 02144

www.candlewick.com

From Here to There

to There

A First Book of Maps

Vivian French

illustrated by

Ya-Ling Huang

CANDLEWICK PRESS

This is Anna's house . . .

and this is where Zane lives.

One day, Zane sent Anna an invitation.

Come over tomorrow!
This will show you the
way to my home.

Love from Zane

It came with a piece of paper.

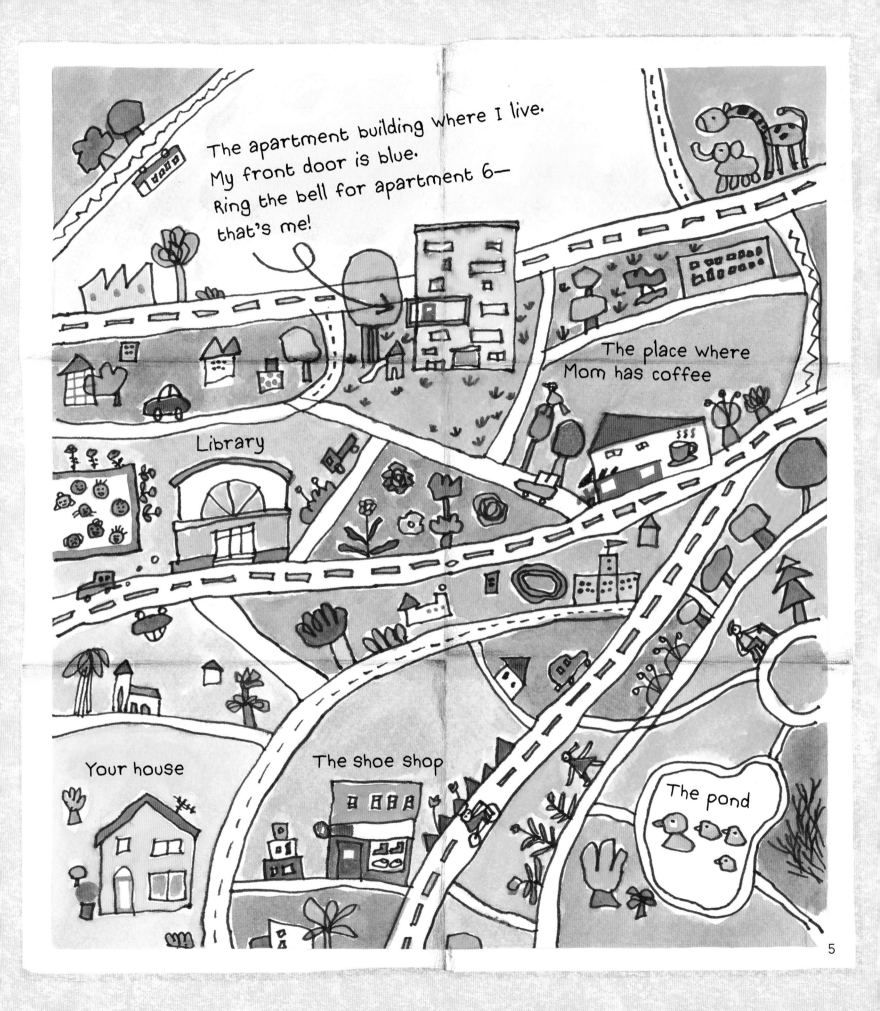

The apartment building where I live.
My front door is blue.
Ring the bell for apartment 6—
that's me!

The place where
Mom has coffee

Library

Your house

The shoe shop

The pond

"Clever Zane," said Dad. "He's drawn you a map, Anna."

"But he's put *his* house in the middle," said Anna, "and our house on the very edge. That's not right."

"Why don't you draw your own map?" Dad went to get some paper. "I'll help you."

"I don't need help," Anna told him. "I can do it!"

You can use a map to help you plan the path you'll follow—your route—from one place to another.

After a little while, Dad came to see how Anna was doing. "I need a lot more paper," she told him. "I can't fit Grandma's house in. She lives too far away."

If you tried to draw everything on a map at its real size, you'd need LOTS of paper—even for just one road!

The size of things on a map, compared to real life, is called the map's scale.

"Maybe you need a different kind of map,"
Dad said. "Look . . .

like this one."

And he unfolded a big sheet.

Anna frowned. "But this map doesn't have real pictures."

"Imagine you're a bird," Dad said, "flying high in the air. This is how you'd see things when you looked down. Those lines are roads—and see this green patch here? That's the park."

There isn't room on this map for lots of words, so instead there are little pictures, or symbols.

Lots of maps have a compass: the N shows you where North is. This is so you don't get the map upside down.

KEY

☕	Café
🏠	Library
🐘	Zoo
☘	Park
═══	Road
▬◻▬	Train tracks

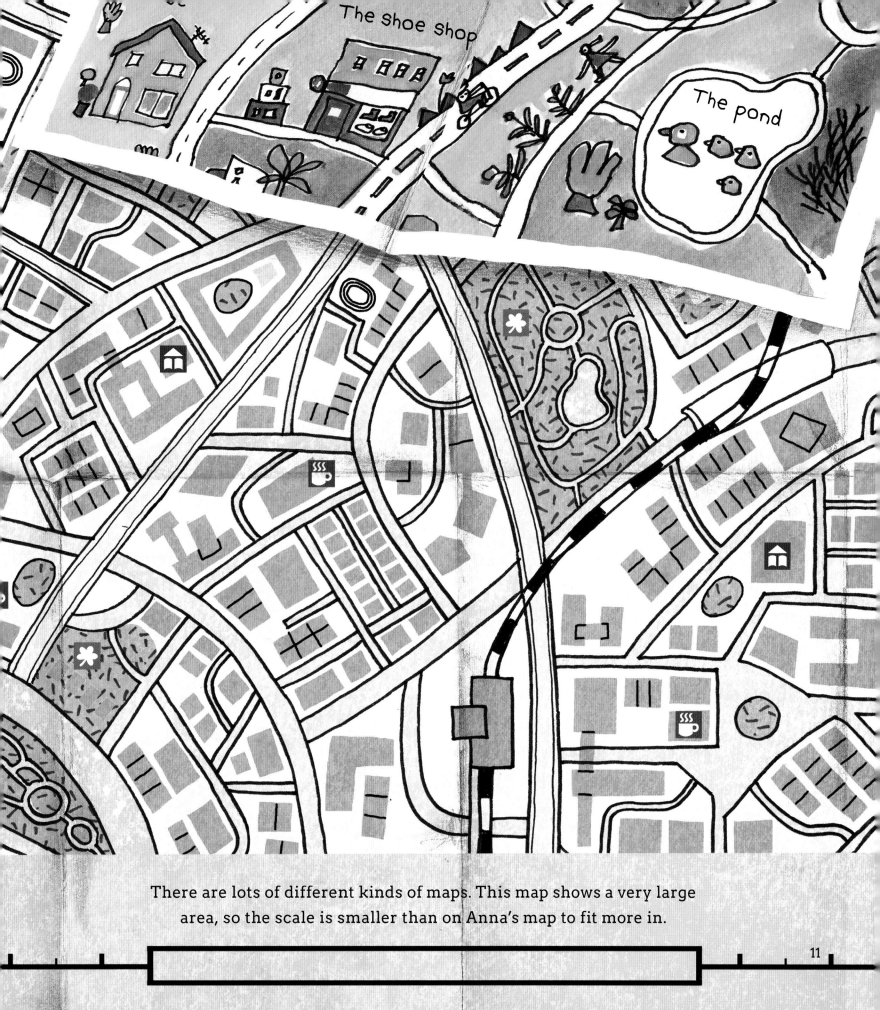

The shoe shop

The pond

There are lots of different kinds of maps. This map shows a very large
area, so the scale is smaller than on Anna's map to fit more in.

Anna peered closely at the map. "What's that little blue part?"

"That's the pond," Dad told her.

"But it doesn't have ducks," Anna said. "Me and Zane drew ducks!"

"No, but this map makes it easier to show places that are far away." Dad picked up a pencil and made two little x's. "Look! That's where our house is . . . and that's Grandma's house."

You can use x's to show where you are on a map and where you want to go.

"I like my map better," Anna said. "I'm going to do another one now for Whiskers."

"A cat map?" Dad laughed. "Show me when you're finished."

Anna drew Whiskers, and then the windowsill . . . the laundry basket (where Whiskers wasn't allowed) . . . Dad's pile of papers . . . Anna's bed . . . the kitchen table . . . the couch . . . and then herself!

Maps are often drawn from above, which is called a bird's-eye view. But, depending on what they're trying to show, they can be drawn from ANY point of view (including Whiskers's!).

End

START

When Dad came back with a drink and a snack, he looked at Anna's cat map.

"I like it! And look," he said, pulling another drawing out of his pocket. "I've made something too."

GRANDMA'S MOM

GRANDMA'S DAD

GRANDDAD'S MOM

GRANDDAD'S DAD

GRANDMA

GRANDDAD

OUR FAMILY

MOM

ANNA

Whiskers

16

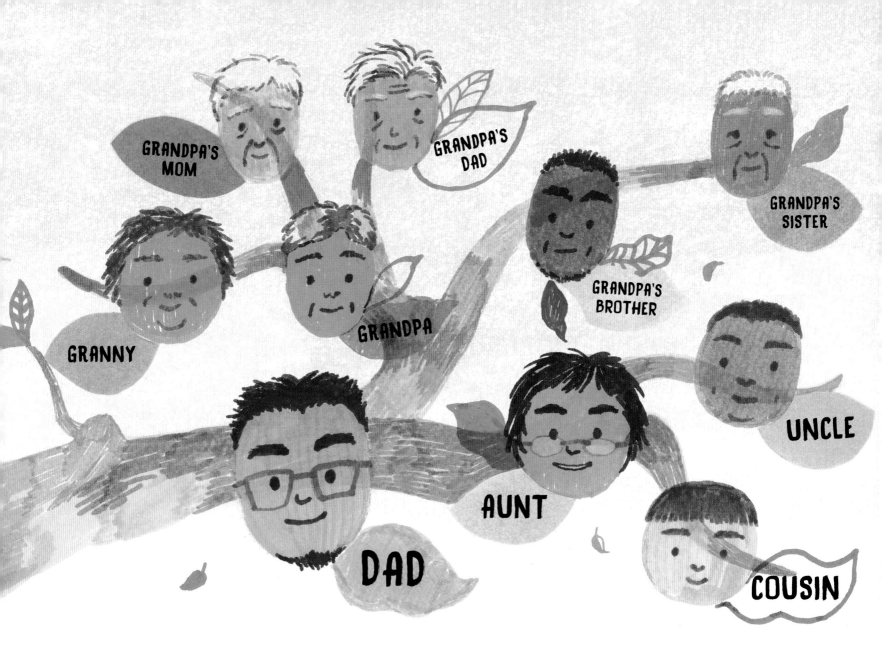

GRANDPA'S MOM

GRANDPA'S DAD

GRANDPA'S SISTER

GRANNY

GRANDPA

GRANDPA'S BROTHER

UNCLE

DAD

AUNT

COUSIN

"This is a completely different kind of map!" Dad told her. "It's called a family tree, and it shows you all the members of your family. Here's you, here's me, and here's Mom . . . Have I forgotten anyone?"

"Whiskers!" Anna said. She drew him in, then picked up another piece of paper.

"What are you up to now?" Dad asked.

"I've got to draw a map for Zane," Anna told him, "so he knows where to come when he visits ME. He can come, can't he?"

Come over tomorrow!
This will show you the way to my home
Love from Zane
Your house
The shoe shop
Library
The apartment building where I live.
My front door is blue.
Ring the bell for apartment 6—
that's me!
The place where
Mom has coffee

"Of course," Dad said.

"Good," Anna said. "And this time I'm putting our house right in the middle!"

The next day, when it was time to go to Zane's house, Anna took Dad's hand.

"I'll show you the way!" she said. "I've got Zane's map!"

"Are you sure?" Dad asked.

Anna nodded. Together they walked past the shoe shop, the pond in the park, the café where Zane's mom liked to get coffee, and the library—all the way to Zane's blue front door.

She rang bell 6 . . .

and there was Zane.

"Hello, Anna!" he said.

MAKING YOUR OWN MAP

Why not make a map of your own? It could be a map of where you live, or you could copy Zane and Anna, and make a map for a friend!

There are lots of different kinds of maps in this book. Your map doesn't have to be of a real place. What about a map where you meet all the characters from the books that you've read? Who would you see in a deep dark wood? Who might be living in a house made of sticks? Would you need a winding path or a straight one?

And of course, don't forget about treasure maps! A map for a pirate . . . or a map for you. What treasure are you hoping to find?

Some other ideas:

A map of a rabbit's underground world

A map of a dream-vacation island

A map for your pet or your favorite animal

A picture "mapping" all the people you know

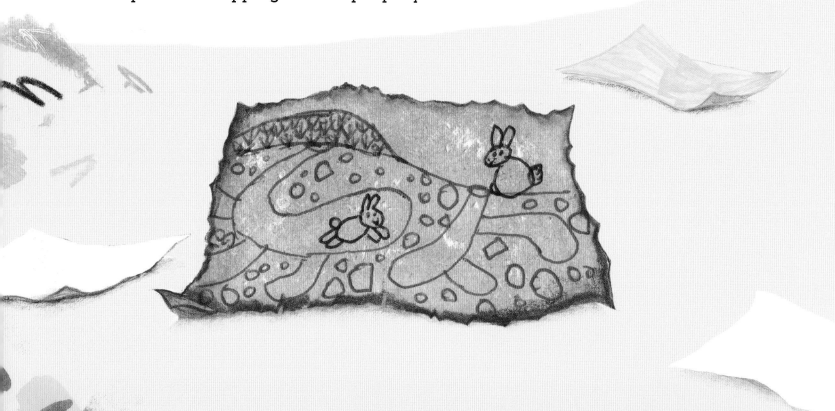

Think about HOW you'd like to draw your map: the best way to include everything you want to show and the best way to decorate it.

Long ago, mapmakers used to add sea monsters or strange animals to their maps to make them more interesting; you could do the same.

And don't forget that your map can be any size or shape you like. It could be a square, a circle, long and thin—or even folded like an accordion.

Have fun!

INDEX